MY FIRST PICTURE DICTIONARY

Angela Wilkes
Revised by Sarah Wedderburn
Illustrated by Colin King
Editorial assistance from Nicola Hall
Consultant: Betty Root

TIGER BOOKS INTERNATIONAL
LONDON

Fifi Lily Sam The dogs Grandpa

about

This book is about dragons.

above

The kite is flying above the tree.

accident

Henry has an accident.

across

The dog runs across the park.

actor

This is a famous actor.

add

Alice adds sugar to her tea.

address

This is Henry's address.

adult

Henry is an adult. He is not a child.

When you grow up you become an adult.

Adults look after children.

afraid

The dog is afraid of mice.

after

Tuesday comes after Monday. It follows Monday. It does not come before it.

He arrived after 12 o'clock, later than midnight.

Ben reads after dinner. He reads when dinner is finished.

afternoon

The afternoon is the part of the day that comes after midday and before evening.

Come and spend the afternoon with me.

Tim plays football on Saturday afternoon.

again

Henry has an accident again.

against

Fifi is leaning against the wall.

age

My friend and I are the same age. We are both six.

At what age did you learn to read?

In the Stone Age people lived in caves.

air

The aeroplane is in the air.

airport

The pilot can see the airport.

alarm clock

The alarm clock is ringing. It wakes up Henry.

alive

The mouse is alive. The doll is not.

all

All the mice are pink.

almost

Grandpa has almost finished the puzzle.

alone

Fifi is all alone. No one is with her.

along

Flowers grow along the path.

alphabet

These are all letters of the alphabet.

already

Lily already has a cake.

also

Bill is a man. Ben is also a man. He is a man too.

Give me an apple and also two bananas.

Fifi is not only beautiful, she is also clever.

although

Although I am tired, I want to dance. I am tired, but I still want to dance.

I will come, although I would prefer to stay at home.

always

Henry is always having accidents.

ambulance

The ambulance is coming to take Henry to hospital.

among

The cat is hiding among the birds.

and

Here are Fritz and Hank.

angel

The angel is flying.

angry

Ben is angry with Bill.

animal

These are all animals.

another

Bill takes another cake.

answer

Here is a sum and its answer.
Is the answer right?

ant

The ant is running across the book.

any

I would like some eggs. Do you have any?

Take any cake you like. Take whichever you like.

anybody

Is anybody there? Is somebody there?

anything

There isn't anything here. There's nothing here.

Do you need anything?

anywhere

Have you seen my hat anywhere?

I can't see him anywhere.

apple

Fifi is eating an apple.

apron

Bill is wearing an apron.

argue

Bill and Ben are arguing.

arm

Ben has broken his arm.

army

Bill is in the army.

arrange

Fifi is arranging the flowers.

arrest

The policeman is arresting the burglar.

arrive

The train is arriving.

arrow

Holmes has found an arrow.

artist

The artist is painting.

as

It was raining as we left. It was raining then.

As it is raining, he is staying at home. He is staying at home because it is raining.

Bill is as tall as Ben.

ask

Lily asks for an apple.

asleep

The cat is asleep in the armchair.

astronaut

Here is an astronaut.

at

The children are at school. Bill is at home and Ben is at work.

At seven o'clock Henry gets up.

Ben is good at French.

aunt

Aunt Alice is Mum's sister.

baby

The baby is crying.

back

Henry is scratching his back.

bad

Johnny is a bad boy. He is not good.

The weather is bad today.

Dad is in a bad mood.

She has a bad cold.

bag

Fifi has a bag to carry her shopping in.

b

baker

The baker is baking bread.

ball

Max catches the ball.

balloon

Lily is chasing a balloon.

banana

The man is weighing a big bunch of bananas.

band

The band is playing music.

bank

Alf is on the river bank.

bark

The dog is barking.

basket

The basket is full of apples.

bat

Henry is holding a baseball bat.

bath

The cat is in the bathroom – in the bath!

beach

Fifi is lying on the beach.

beak

The bird has a red beak.

bean

These are green beans.

bear

Bruno is a brown bear.

beard

The man has a long beard.

beautiful

Here is a beautiful princess.

because

The baby is crying because she is hungry. That is the reason she is crying.

Because the sun is shining today, I feel happy.

We must run because we are late.

bed

The king is in bed.

bedroom

The bed is in the bedroom.

bee

The bee is on a flower.

beef

The butcher is carving the beef. Beef is meat from cows.

before

Monday comes before Tuesday. It does not come after it.

I was home before Sam. I got there earlier than him.

Why didn't you tell me before?

begin

It is beginning to rain. It is starting to rain.

The match is beginning.

The film begins at 7 o'clock and ends at 9 o'clock.

I have already begun school.

behind

Who is behind the tree?

believe

Sam believes in ghosts. He thinks they really exist.

Sam believes anything you tell him. He thinks everything you tell him is true.

Do you believe in God?

bell

The bell is ringing.

belong

That bicycle belongs to me. It is mine.

The hat belongs to Ben. It is Ben's hat.

Ben belongs to a club. He is one of its members.

below

The cat is sitting below Bruno on the stairs.

belt

Fifi is wearing a big belt.

bench

The bird is on the bench.

bend

Sam is bending a spoon.

best

Fifi is the best dancer. She is a better dancer than anyone else.

Who is your best friend?

Do your best. Try as hard as you can.

better

Fifi is a better dancer than Susie. Susie is a good dancer but Fifi is a very good dancer.

Henry speaks French better than Ben.

I was ill yesterday but I feel better now.

between

The cat is sitting between the two bears.

bicycle

The baker is riding a bicycle.

big

The elephant is big.

bird

The bird is riding a bicycle.

birthday

It is Lily's birthday today.

bite

The dog is biting the postman.

black

The big cat is black.

blackbird

A blackbird is black.

blackboard

Ben is writing on the blackboard.

blanket

There is a red blanket on the bed.

blind

A dog is leading the blind man.

blood

Sam has blood on his finger.

blow

Lily is blowing out the candles.

bonfire

The bonfire is burning.

bottle

Fifi has a bottle of orange juice.

blue

The house is blue.

book

The book is about boats.

bottom

The frog is at the bottom of the ladder.

boat

Three men are in the boat.

bookshop

Bill looks in the bookshop.

bowl

The bowl is full of bananas.

body

Sam has a strong body.

boot

The bird is wearing a blue boot.

box

The cat is asleep in a box.

bone

Max has a big bone.

both

Both of the pigs are pink.

boy

Tom is a little boy.

bracelet

Lily is wearing a blue bracelet.

branch

The bird is standing on the branch of a tree.

bread

Bill is cutting the bread.

break

Ben breaks the bread in half.

breakfast

Fifi has her breakfast.

breathe

Fish can breathe underwater.

brick

The builder is carrying a brick.

bride

Here comes the bride . . .

bridegroom

. . . and here is her bridegroom.

bridge

Bill crosses the bridge.

bright

The star is bright.

bring

Max brings Bill a slipper.

brother

Bill and Ben are brothers.

brown

Bruno is a brown bear.

brush

Fritz is brushing his shoes.

bubble

Bruno is blowing a bubble.

bucket

Bill empties the bucket.

bud

The plant has one bud.

build

The builder is building a house.

building

A house is a building.

bulb

The caterpillar is looking at the flower bulb.

bull

The angry bull is chasing Bill.

bulldozer

Ben drives a bulldozer.

bump

Henry has hit a bump.

bunch

The flowers are all together in a big bunch.

burn

The house is burning!

bus

The bus is stopping.

bus stop

Fifi is waiting at the bus stop.

busy

The man is busy. He has a lot of work to do.

but

Bill eats a lot, but he is not fat.

I like sweets, but I do not like chocolate.

I want a new dress, but I have no money.

butcher

The butcher sells meat.

butter

The butter is melting.

butterfly

The bee meets a butterfly

buy

Fifi buys some bananas. She pays money for them.

by

The man is standing by the car.

cabbage

Fifi chooses a cabbage.

café

The friends are going to a café.

cage

The lion is in a cage.

cake

Fifi is cutting the cake.

calculator

The man is using his calculator.

calendar

Alice is looking at the calendar.

calf

The calf is with its mother.

call

The farmer calls the calf. He shouts to it.

camel

Henry is riding a camel.

camera

Bill has a new camera.

camp

Bill and Ben are camping.

can

Sam is opening a can of beans.

candle

Henry is carrying a candle.

cap

Henry is wearing a green cap.

capital

Rome is the capital of Italy. It is the country's main city.

Paris is the capital of France.

'A' is a capital letter and 'a' is a small letter.

car

Fred has a fast car.

card

The men are playing a game of cards.

careful

Henry should be more careful!

carpet

The carpet is blue.

carrot

The man is holding a bunch of carrots.

carry

Lily is carrying the carrots.

castle

The castle is on a hill.

cat

The cat is lying on the carpet.

catch

The cat catches the ball. The mouse threw it to him.

caterpillar

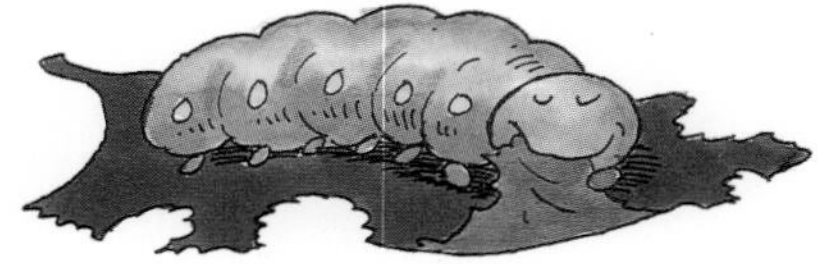

The caterpillar is eating a leaf.

cauliflower

The caterpillar has found a cauliflower in a basket.

cave

There is treasure in the cave.

ceiling

Sam can reach the ceiling.

cellar

The cellar is full of bottles.

chain

Grandpa has a watch on a chain.

chair

Bruno is sitting on a chair.

chalk

Bruno is writing with chalk on a blackboard.

change

Bill is counting his change.

change

Henry is changing a wheel.

chase

The dog is chasing a rabbit.

cheap

The armchair is cheap. It does not cost much.

check

Grandpa checks the time.

cheek

Alice has pink cheeks.

cheese

Fifi is eating cheese.

cherry

A bird is eating the cherries.

chest

Sam is beating his chest.

chick

The hen has five chicks.

chicken

Ben is cutting the chicken.

child, children

The children are playing.

chimney

The bird is sitting on a chimney.

chimpanzee

The chimpanzee is swinging from a tree.

chin

Sam is rubbing his chin.

chocolate

Lily is eating chocolate.

choose

Fifi chooses a green dress. She picks it out.

chop

Ben has a chop for dinner.

chop

Sam is chopping wood.

Christmas

It is Christmas. Father Christmas is here.

church

Fifi is going to church.

circle

The chicks are going round in a circle.

circus

The people are watching a clown at the circus.

city

A city is a very big town. Many people live there.

clap

Fifi and Sam clap their hands at the end of the show.

class

There are five children in the class.

classroom

The classroom is empty.

clean

Bill puts on a clean apron. The other one is dirty.

clean

Henry is cleaning his car.

clever

Brains is clever. He learns fast.

cliff

Henry is standing on a cliff.

climb

Sam is climbing up the cliff.

clock

Ben is cleaning the clock.

close

Fifi closes the window.

clothes

Fifi looks in the wardrobe to find her clothes.

cloud

The angel is lying on a cloud.

clown

This clown is wearing a red nose.

coast

Trees grow along the coast. The coast is by the sea.

coat

The king's coat is too big.

cobweb

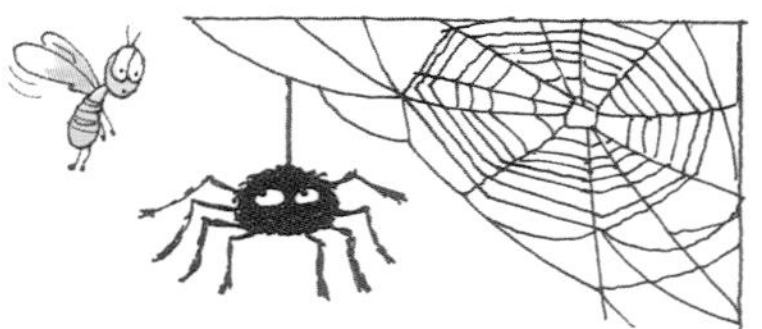

The spider makes a cobweb.

coffee

Fifi pours the coffee.

coin

Fifi puts coins in her purse.

cold

Oscar is cold. He is not warm.

collect

Bill has a lot of badges. He collects them.

colour

There are seven colours in the rainbow.

comb

Fifi has a big comb.

comb

Fifi combs her hair with her comb.

come

The duck is coming towards Lily.

comfortable

Fifi is very comfortable in her bed.

comic

The boys are reading a comic.

computer

Brains is working on a computer.

conductor

Herbert is a conductor. He conducts an orchestra.

cook

Henry is cooking dinner.

cool

Ben puts milk in the fridge to keep it cool.

cork

The cork pops out of the bottle.

corner

Ruff is sitting in the corner.

cost

Diamonds cost a lot of money. They are expensive.

What does it cost to go on the bus? How much money must I pay?

cough

Fifi is coughing.

count

Lily is counting the cakes to see how many there are.

country

England is a small country.

China and India are big countries.

How many countries are there in the world?

country

Jack lives in the country, not in a town.

cover

Bill covers his head with a newspaper.

cow

The cow has a friend on its back.

cowboy

The cowboy is chasing a cow.

crab

The crab runs sideways.

crane

The crane is lifting a car.

crayon

Lily draws with crayons.

cream

There is cream on the cake.

crocodile

The crocodile seems to be asleep.

cross

Two mice are dancing on a red cross.

cross

The hedgehog is crossing the road.

crown

The king wears a crown.

cry

Fifi is crying because the film is sad.

cube

A cube has six sides.

cucumber

The mice are carrying a cucumber.

cup

The caterpillar looks in the cup.

cupboard

The cup is in the cupboard.

curtain

Fifi opens the curtains.

cushion

The crown is on a cushion.

customer

The customer is buying bread from the baker.

cut

Fifi is cutting Ben's hair.

cut out

Fifi is cutting out a picture.

dance

Fifi is dancing with Sam.

dancer

She would like to be a famous dancer.

danger

Help! The bee is in danger!

dare

The man does not dare dive. He is afraid to dive.

dark

The room is dark. It is not light.

daughter

Lily is Mary's daughter. Mary is Lily's mother.

day

There are 365 days in a year.

There are seven days in a week: Sunday, Monday, Tuesday, Wednesday, Thursday, Friday and Saturday.

There are 24 hours in a day.

dead

Ruff is pretending to be dead but he is really alive.

deaf

Grandpa is deaf. He cannot hear well.

decide

Bill decides to buy a car. He makes up his mind to buy one.

Decide which dress you want. Make up your mind which one you want.

I can't decide what to do today.

deep

Fifi is in deep water.

deer

Max meets a deer.

deliver

The postman is delivering a parcel to Alice.

dentist

The dentist is looking at Henry's teeth.

describe

Shall I describe my friend to you? Shall I tell you what she looks like?

Describe this place to me. Tell me what it is like.

desert

Camels live in the desert.

desk

Jake is working at his desk.

dictionary

Fritz has a dictionary. It tells him what words mean.

die

Henry's plant is dying. Soon it will be dead.

different

The men are wearing different hats.

difficult

It is difficult for the porter to carry all the suitcases.

dig

Dan is digging with a spade.

dining room

The mice are eating in the dining room.

dinner

The monster is eating his dinner.

dinosaur

The dinosaur is eating his dinner.

direction

Max is changing direction. He is going to go the other way.

dirty

The dinosaur is dirty.

dish

Here is a dish of strawberries.

do

Henry is doing nothing.

doctor

The doctor is examining Sam to see if he is ill.

dog

The dog is going for a walk with Mark.

doll

Lily is playing with a doll.

donkey

Henry is riding a donkey.

door

Fifi shuts the door.

dragon

The dragon is breathing fire.

draw

Fifi is drawing a dragon.

drawing

This is her drawing.

dream

Henry dreams about spiders when he is asleep.

dress

Fifi is wearing a long dress.

dress

Fifi is dressing Lily. She is putting on her clothes.

drink

Sam is drinking milk.

drip

Why is water dripping on the mat?

drive

Henry is driving a lorry.

driver

He is a good driver.

drop

Henry drops an egg.

drum

Fred is playing his drum.

dry

The ground is very dry because it has not rained.

duck

The duck is in the bath.

dust

Max is rolling in the dust.

each

Each child has a cake.

eagle

The eagle is in its nest.

ear

The donkey has long ears.

early

Ben gets up early in the morning. He does not get up late.

I am coming home early. I am coming home sooner than I usually do.

The shops close early on Monday.

earth

The earth is round.

east

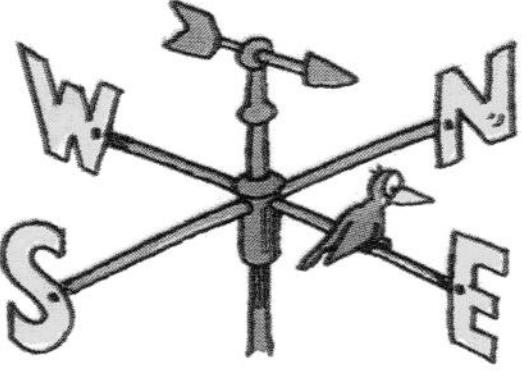

The bird is facing east. East is opposite west.

Easter

Easter is a religious holiday in the spring.

People do not go to work on Good Friday or Easter Monday.

easy

It is easy to make a cake. It is not difficult.

Joe's homework is easy.

I can easily finish my work in an hour.

eat

Lily is eating chocolate.

edge

Lily is sitting on the edge of the table.

egg

Lily is eating an egg for breakfast.

elbow

Henry hits his elbow.

elephant

The elephant is sitting down.

empty

Henry is emptying the bucket.

end

The mouse is swinging at the end of the rope.

enough

Fifi has enough money to buy a new car. She has as much money as she needs to buy it.

Have you had enough to eat? Have you had as much as you want?

enter

The king enters the room.

entrance

Henry is standing at the entrance to a cave.

envelope

Fifi is opening the envelope.

escape

The prisoner escapes from the castle.

evening

The sun sets in the evening and it gets dark.

every

Every pig is pink. They are all the same colour.

everyone

Everyone is wearing a hat. Each person has one.

everything

Everything in this shop is expensive. All the things are expensive.

everywhere

Fifi looks everywhere for her cat. She looks in every place.

except

Every pig is pink except for one.

exciting

Jake is reading an exciting book. It is a thriller.

experiment

Brains does an experiment to see what will happen.

explain

Fifi explains why she wants a car. She makes it clear why she wants it.

Can you explain what happened?

Explain to me how it works.

eye

The cat has blue eyes.

fabric

Fifi is sewing a button onto some fabric.

face

Fifi is washing her face.

fact

It is a fact that the earth is round. It is true.

The dog looked fierce but in fact he was very friendly.

factory

This man works in a factory where cars are made.

fairy

The fairy is sitting on a flower.

fall

The fairy falls off the flower.

family

There are three people in Fifi's family.

famous

Will is a famous artist. He is well known.

fan

Fifi is fanning herself with a fan.

far

Ben is far from the house. He is not near to it.

farm

The farm is in the country.

farmer

The farmer lives in the farmhouse.

fast

The farmer runs fast.

fat

The sheep is eating lots of grass. It is getting fat.

father

Lily is with her father. She is his daughter.

favourite

Chips are Ben's favourite food. He likes them best.

feather

The bird has yellow feathers.

feed

Lily is feeding the ducks.

feel

Bill can feel the chair. He is touching it.

feet

Here are two big feet.

fence

The cow is jumping over the fence.

few

This bird has few feathers. It does not have many.

field

The cows are in a field.

fight

Bill and Ben are fighting.

fill

Fifi fills the glass with milk.

find

Bill finds the book he was looking for.

finger

Lily is licking her fingers.

finish

Fifi finishes her dinner. She eats all of it.

fire

The men are sitting by the fire to keep warm.

fireman

The firemen put out the fire.

fireworks

Look at the fireworks!

first

Bill is first in the queue. Who is last?

fish

A big fish meets a little fish.

fish

John is fishing. He wants to catch fish.

flag

Henry is carrying a flag.

flame

Lily blows out the flame.

flat

This house has a flat roof.

floor

Ruff is lying on the floor.

flour

Bill uses flour to make a cake.

flow

The river flows towards the sea.

flower

Henry gives Fifi a flower.

flowerbed

The flowers are planted in a flowerbed.

fly

There is a fly on the flower.

fly

The fly is flying away.

fog

Henry cannot see much in the fog. He is lost.

follow

Henry is following a dog.

food

Jake has lots of food to eat.

for

The present is for Ben.

forehead

Henry hits his forehead.

forest

Many trees grow in a forest.

forget

Bill always forgets my name. He does not remember it.

I have forgotten where he lives.

Don't forget to come!

fork

Ben has a fork in his hand.

forwards

The lorry is going forwards. It is not going backwards.

fox

The fox is running down the hill.

free

The mouse does not live in a cage, it lives in the woods. It is free.

The ticket is free. It does not cost anything.

freeze

When water freezes it turns into ice.

The pond freezes over in winter.

You can freeze food in a freezer.

friend

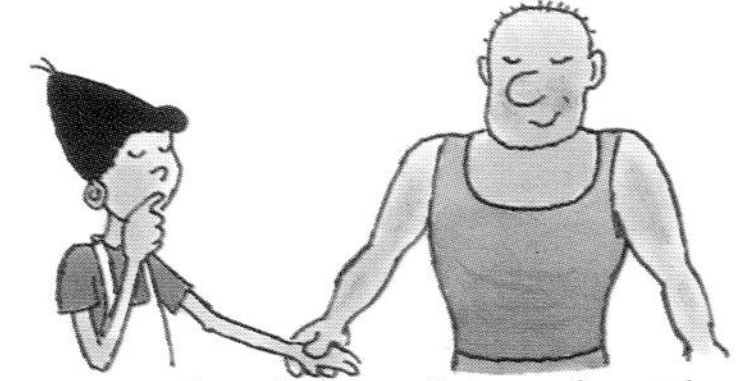

Sam and Fifi are friends. They like each other.

frighten

Fifi frightens her friend.

frog

The frog is jumping.

from

The letter is from Germany. It is from Fritz to Henry.

Pierre comes from France.

I live ten miles from London.

front

Ben is in front of Bill in the queue.

frost

There is frost on the window. It was cold last night.

fruit

These are all different kinds of fruit.

fry

Ben is frying an egg.

frying pan

You fry eggs in a frying pan.

full

The bath is full of water.

funfair

Fifi is having fun at the funfair.

funny

The clown is funny. He makes people laugh.

fur

The rabbit has white fur. Its fur is soft.

gate

The farmer shuts the gate.

girl

The little girl is running after the cat.

game

The children are playing a game of blindman's buff.

get up

Ben gets up at 8 o'clock.

give

The girl gives Ben a flower.

garage

The car is in the garage.

ghost

The ghost touches Henry.

glass

The glass is full of milk.

garden

Flowers grow in the garden.

giant

A giant is a very big person.

glasses

Henry is wearing glasses to help him read.

gas

Henry lights the gas.

giraffe

The giraffe is eating leaves.

glove

Sam is wearing a pair of leather gloves.

go

The children are going to school.

goat

The goat is biting Henry.

gold

The king's cup is made of gold.

good

This baker makes good bread. He is a good baker.

goose

The goose is hissing at the goat.

grape

Here is a bunch of grapes.

grapefruit

Fifi is eating a grapefruit.

grass

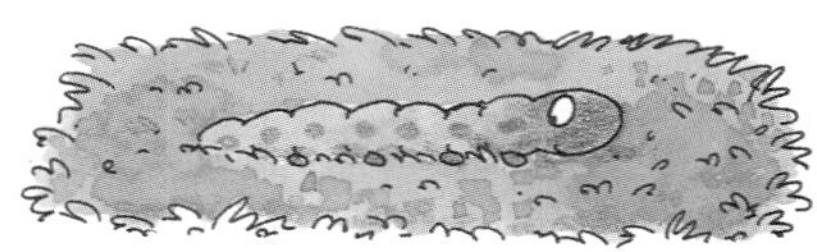

The grass is green.

green

Everything on the table is green.

grocer

The grocer sells food.

ground

Henry drives his van over bumpy ground.

group

Here is a group of boys.

grow

Lily is growing. She is getting taller.

guest

Fifi welcomes her guest. He is coming to dinner.

guitar

Manuel is playing the guitar.

hair

Grandma has white hair.

hairbrush

She brushes her hair with a pink hairbrush.

hairdresser

The hairdresser is cutting Fifi's hair.

half

Lily has one half of the orange. Fifi has the other half.

ham

Bill is cutting the ham.

hamburger

Sam has two hamburgers.

hammer

Henry is using a hammer.

hand

Henry hits his hand with the hammer.

handbag

Fifi is emptying her handbag.

handkerchief

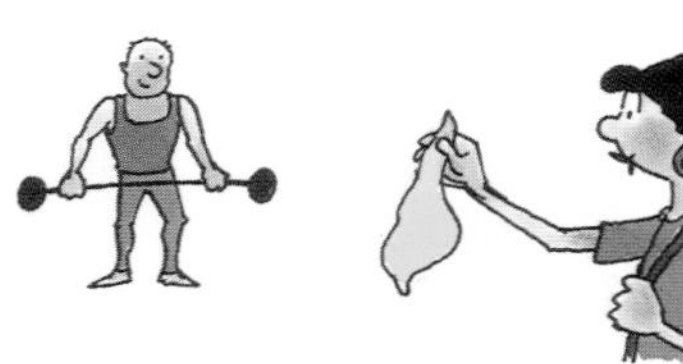

Fifi is waving her handkerchief.

handle

The handle of the cup breaks.

hang

Henry is hanging from the edge of the cliff.

happen

Where did the accident happen? Where did it take place?

I didn't think this would happen!

What's happened to him?

happy

Bill is happy to see Ben. He is pleased to see him.

harbour

The boats are in the harbour.

hard

The mattress is hard. It is not soft.

hat

Fifi is wearing a pretty hat.

have

Bill and Ben have two cats. The cats belong to them.

hay

The farmer cuts grass to make hay.

head

Henry has a bird on his head.

hear

Grandpa cannot hear well.

heart

The heart is the muscle that pumps blood round your body.

When you run, your heart beats faster.

I love you with all my heart.

heat

Ben has been heating some soup in a pan.

heavy

The rock is heavy. It is not light.

hedge

Henry is cutting the hedge.

helicopter

The helicopter is flying.

help

Bill is helping Ben move the piano.

hen

The hen is eating seeds.

here

Come here. Come to this place where I am standing.

Put the chair here, not there.

Do you live here, in this house?

Here we are!

hide

The cat is hiding under the aeroplane.

high

This mountain is very high.

hill

The house is on a hill.

hippopotamus

This hippopotamus has been playing in the mud.

hit

Henry hits a nail with his hammer.

hold

Henry is holding the rope. He is not letting go.

hole

Ruff is digging a hole.

home

Fred lives in a caravan. It is his home.

homework

Joe is doing the homework his teacher has given him.

hook

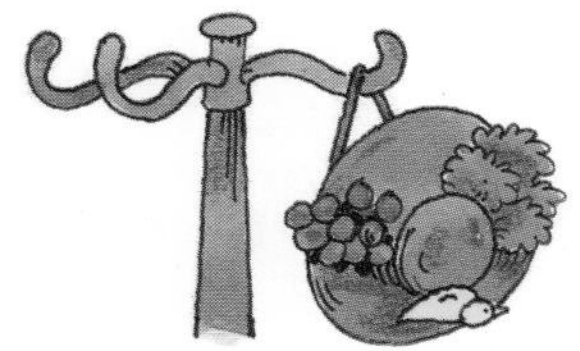

The hat is hanging on a hook.

hop

The rabbit hops over Ruff.

hope

We are not sure that we can go to Paris, but we are hoping to go.

I hope you are well.

Fifi hopes that she will be a famous dancer one day.

horse

Henry is riding a horse.

hospital

Henry is in hospital.

hot

The soup is hot. It is not cold.

hot dog

The girls are eating hot dogs.

hotel

Fifi is going to a hotel for a holiday.

hour

There are 24 hours in a day.

There are 60 minutes in an hour.

Ben works eight hours a day.

It takes me half an hour to get home.

house

Fritz lives in a big house.

how

I know how to make a cake. I know what you have to do.

How are you?

How do you say that in French?

hug

Fritz hugs Heidi.

hungry

Lily is hungry. She wants something to eat.

hurry

Henry is hurrying. He is running fast.

hurt

Poor Henry! He has hurt his foot.

husband

Fritz is Heidi's husband. He is married to her.

ice

The pond is covered with ice.

ice cream

Lily is eating an ice cream.

idea

Henry has an idea about what to do on his birthday. He has thought of something to do.

I have a good idea! I have thought of something good.

I have no idea where Ben is.

if

If you ask him, he will tell you. Ask him and he will tell you.

Fifi asks if Sam is at home. "Is Sam at home?" she asks.

Come if you can, but not if you're too busy.

ill

Bill is ill. He does not feel well.

important

Prime Ministers are important people. They have a lot of power.

It is important that you brush your teeth every day.

It doesn't matter. It's not important.

in

The cat is in its basket.

ink

Fifi has spilt ink on the table.

insect

Which one of these creatures is not really an insect?

instead

Bill is going to the shop instead of Ben. Bill is going in place of Ben.

Fifi eats honey instead of sugar.

He is playing instead of working.

invite

Fifi has invited 20 people to her party. She has asked 20 people to come.

We are invited to dinner at the palace. The king has sent an invitation.

iron

This is an iron.

iron

Henry is ironing his shirt.

island

An island is land surrounded by water.

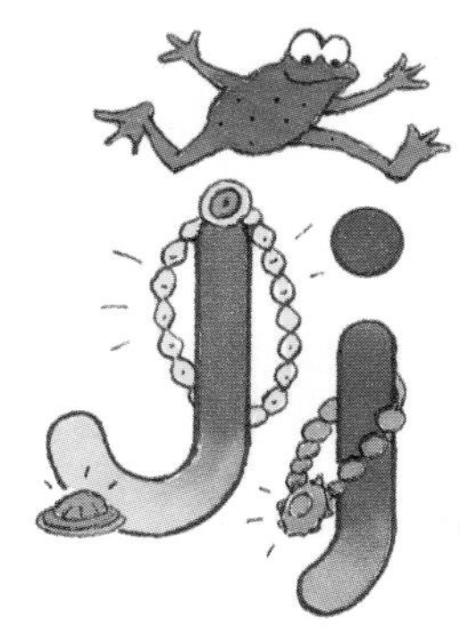

jacket

Fritz has a green jacket.

jam

Here is a jar of strawberry jam.

jar

The jar is empty.

jeans

This is a pair of jeans.

jewels

The chest is full of precious jewels.

join

Bill is joining two wires together.

joke

Bill tells Ben a joke to make him laugh.

journey

The clowns are on a journey. They are travelling.

jump

One frog is jumping over the other frog.

kangaroo

A kangaroo jumps over Fred.

keep

Lily wants to keep the kitten. She wants to have it for ever.

Can I keep the penny I found?

Keep going. Do not stop.

My coat keeps me warm.

kettle

The kettle is boiling.

key

George has a key to open the door.

kick

Sam kicks the ball.

kill

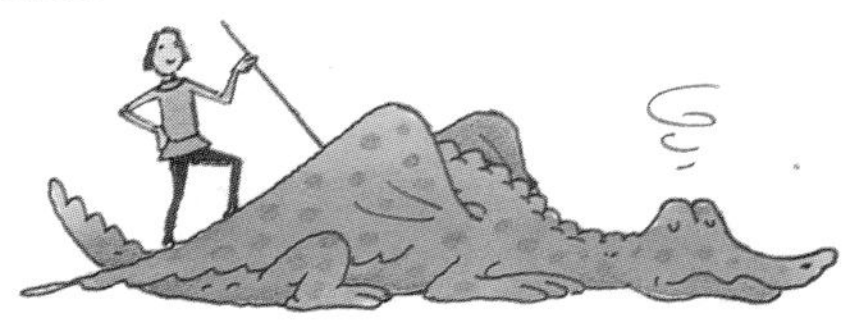

The prince has killed the dragon. It is dead.

kind

An apple is a kind of fruit. It is a sort of fruit.

An onion is a kind of vegetable.

What kind of cake is it?

kind

Jim is kind to animals. He is gentle with them.

king

The king is wearing a crown.

kiss

Fifi is kissing Sam.

kitchen

Ben cooks in the kitchen.

kite

Bill is flying a kite.

kitten

A kitten is a baby cat.

knee

Henry falls on his knee.

knife

Bill cuts bread with a knife.

knit

Henry is knitting.

knock

Sam knocks at the door.

knot

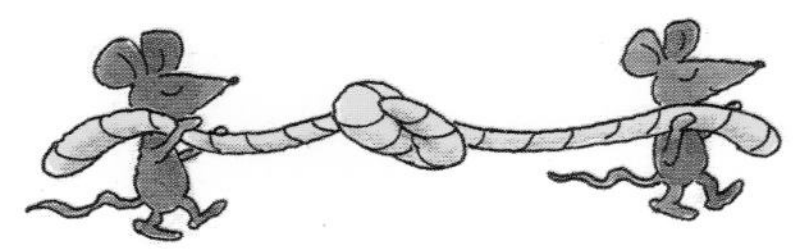

The string has a knot in it.

know

Fritz knows how to swim. He can swim.

I know that two and two makes four. I have learnt it.

Sam knows Ben. He has met him.

lace

The dress is made of lace.

ladder

Henry climbs the ladder.

lake

There are boats on the lake.

lamb

A lamb is a baby sheep.

lamp

Fifi is reading by the lamp.

lawn

Fifi is mowing the lawn.

lean

Bruno is leaning on a fence.

last

Ben is last in the queue. Who is first?

lazy

Mark is lazy. He does not like working.

learn

Fifi is learning how to drive. She is finding out how to drive.

You learn things at school.

I am learning French.

A teacher helps you to learn.

last

The film lasts an hour. It goes on for an hour.

The rain lasted for five days.

This loaf of bread won't last long. You ate half on the way home!

lead

Ben is leading the children. He shows them the way.

leather

This bag is made of leather. Leather is animal skin.

late

Tim is late for school. He is not on time.

He goes to bed late, not early.

It is too late now to go for a walk.

leaf

The ant is carrying a leaf.

leave

Fifi is leaving the house. She is going away.

laugh

Ben is laughing. He is laughing at Bill.

leak

Ben's tap is leaking. Water is dripping from it all the time.

left

Fritz is turning left.

leg

Henry is skating on one leg.

lemon

Fifi is cutting a lemon in half.

less

I have less cake than you. You have more than me.

Henry is less strong than Sam. He is not as strong.

He left less than an hour ago.

lesson

The class is having a lesson. They are learning.

letter

Sam is reading a letter.

lettuce

The caterpillar likes lettuce.

library

Bill borrows books from the library.

lick

Lily is licking her ice cream.

lid

Bill is putting the lid on the jar.

lie

Bill says he never eats sweets. He is telling a lie. He is not telling the truth.

lie

Bill is lying. He says he has two birthdays this year.

lie

Ruff is lying in his kennel.

life

Butterflies have a short life. They do not live long.

He saved my life. He stopped me from dying.

I have known her all my life.

lift

The crane is lifting a car.

light

George has put the light on.

light

The dancer is light. She is not heavy.

light

Fritz lights a match.

lighthouse

The lighthouse is by the sea.

lightning

Lightning flashes in the sky.

like

Fifi likes Ben. He is her friend.

like

I wish I could dance like Fifi. I wish I could dance as she dances.

Sam swims like a fish.

You do it like this. This is how you do it.

lion

The lion is roaring.

list

Henry is writing a long list.

listen

Grandpa is listening to the radio.

live

Rob lives on an island. His home is there.

living room

This is a living room.

long

The snake is long. It is not short.

look

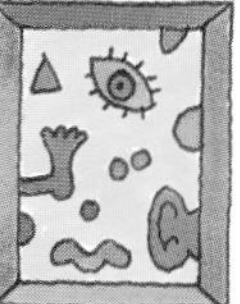

Fifi is looking at the picture.

look for

Henry is looking for a book. He is trying to find it.

lose

Bill loses things. Today he cannot find the fish.

lost

Henry is lost. He does not know where he is.

lot

A lot of birds are in the tree.

loud

The band plays loud music. It is very noisy.

love

Sam loves Fifi.

low

The wall is low. It is not high.

lunch

Lily eats lunch at midday.

machine

All these machines work.

magazine

Henry is reading a magazine.

magician

The magician has just done a trick.

mail

The postman brings the mail.

make

Ben is making a cake.

man

There are three people in this picture, two women and one man.

many

There are many magazines on this bookstall.

map

Henry is looking at a map to see where to go.

mark

There is a mark on the map.

market

This is a market. You can buy things here.

marry

Sam is marrying Fifi.

mask

Who is wearing the mask?

measure

Fifi measures Lily to find out how tall she is.

meat

The butcher is chopping meat.

medicine

The nurse is giving Lily medicine to make her better.

meet

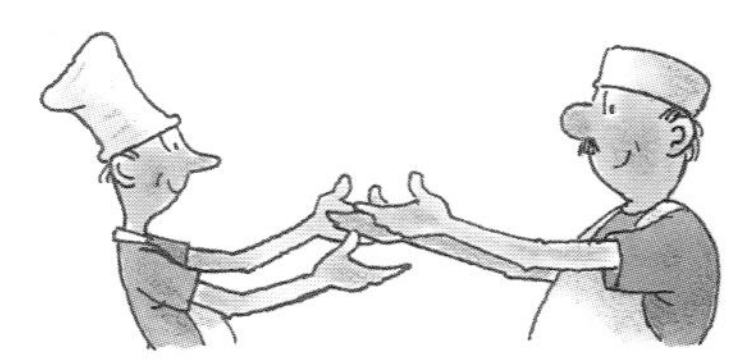

Bill and Ben meet.

melt

The ice cream is melting.

menu

Sam and Fifi read the menu so they can decide what to eat.

metal

Cars are made of metal.

middle

The pig is in the middle.

milk

Lily is drinking milk.

minute

There are 60 seconds in a minute, and 60 minutes in an hour.

Ben likes his egg boiled for four minutes.

Wait a minute!

mirror

The cat is looking at himself in the mirror.

mischief

Lily is up to mischief. She is supposed to be asleep.

miss

Henry has missed the bus.

model

Fritz is making a model aeroplane.

money

Ben is counting his money.

monkey

The monkey is swinging from a tree.

monster

This monster is friendly.

month

There are twelve months in the year: January, February, March, April, May, June, July, August, September, October, November and December.

moon

The moon shines in the sky at night.

more

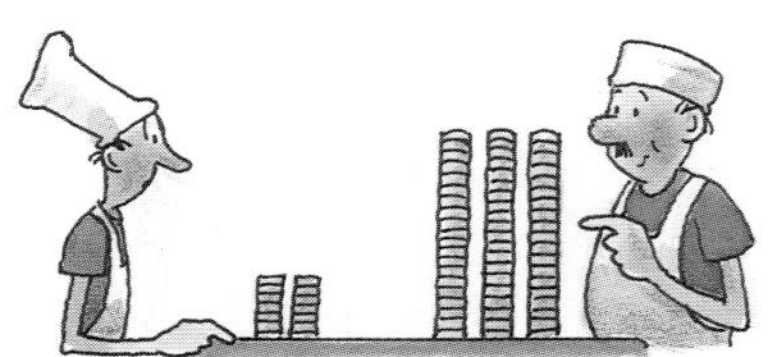

Bill has more money than Ben.

morning

Morning is the part of the day before midday.

We get up in the morning.

People go to work and school in the morning.

most

Most of the apples are red. Nearly all of them are red.

mother

Mary is Lily's mother. Lily is her daughter.

motorbike

Henry is riding a motorbike.

mountain

There is snow on the top of this mountain.

mouse, mice

One mouse is pink. The other mice are brown.

mouth

This man has a big mouth.

move

Bill and Ben are moving the table.

much

Do you have much money? Do you have a lot of money?

I feel much better today. I feel a lot better.

You are making too much noise.

mud

This monster likes mud.

mushroom

The mouse is dancing on the mushroom.

music

This music sounds good!

name

Lily has written her name.

naughty

Lily is being naughty. She is not being good.

near

The tree is near the house. It is close to the house.

neck

A giraffe has a long neck.

necklace

Fifi is wearing a necklace.

need

Lily needs a bath because she is dirty.

needle

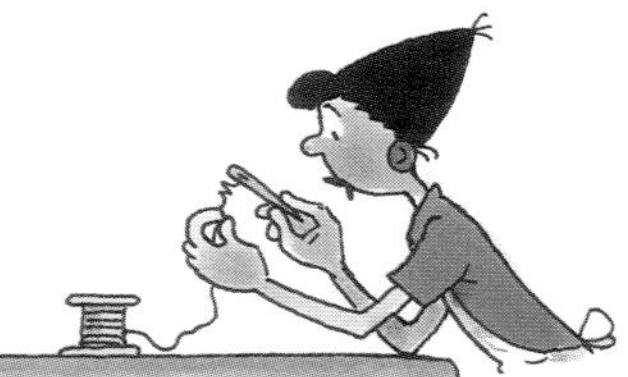

Fifi is threading a needle.

nest

The baby birds are in their nest.

never

Fifi never eats cheese. She does not eat cheese at any time.

I never watch television.

Grandpa never goes out.

I have never been to France.

new

Ben has a new car. It is not old.

newspaper

Bill is reading a newspaper.

next

Fifi is sitting next to Sam.

night

Night is the part of the day when the sky is dark.

At night people go to sleep.

Every night, before I go to bed, I have my supper.

Good night!

nobody

Nobody is wearing a hat.

noise

Lily is making a noise.

north

The bird is facing north. North is opposite south.

nose

Henry's nose is red.

not

The angel is not flying.

notebook

The man is looking at his notebook.

nothing

There is nothing in the box. It is empty.

now

Come here now, not later! Come here this minute!

Fifi was here this morning but she is not here now.

Ben must be at home by now.

It is now six o'clock.

number

These are all numbers.

nurse

The nurse is looking after Ben because he is ill.

nut

Lily is eating nuts.

octopus

The octopus lives in the sea.

offer

Sam offers Fifi flowers. He is giving them to her.

office

Jake works in an office.

often

The telephone often rings. It rings many times a day.

oil

Joe puts oil on his bicycle. He is oiling it.

old

Grandpa is an old man. He is not young.

on

The cup is on the table.

onion

Henry is slicing an onion.

only

There is only one banana left. There were three, but now there is just one.

Only two of the roses are red. The rest are pink.

My friend is nine, but I am only six.

open

The shop is open. People can go into it.

open

Fifi opens the door to the postman.

opposite

Hot is the opposite of cold.

or

Which shoes do you want? The blue ones or the red ones? You must choose one of the two pairs.

Shall we walk or cycle?

You can either sit here or there.

orange

An orange is a kind of fruit.

orange

Henry has orange socks.

orchard

This is a cherry orchard.

orchestra

The orchestra is giving a concert.

order

Fritz orders dinner. He tells the waiter what to bring.

other

Where is Henry's other sock?

out

The toys are out of the box. They are not in it.

outside

Lily is playing outside. She is not inside.

over

The pig is jumping over the fence.

overflow

The basin is overflowing. Water is running over the top.

owl

The owl is sitting in the tree.

Pp

page

This is the first page of the book.

paint

The artist is painting a picture.

paints

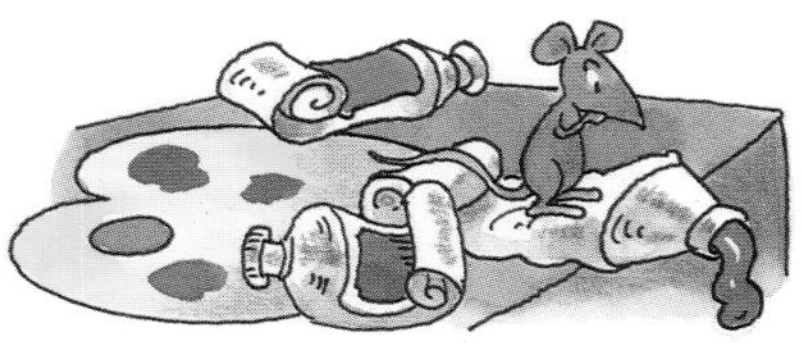

These are her paints.

pair

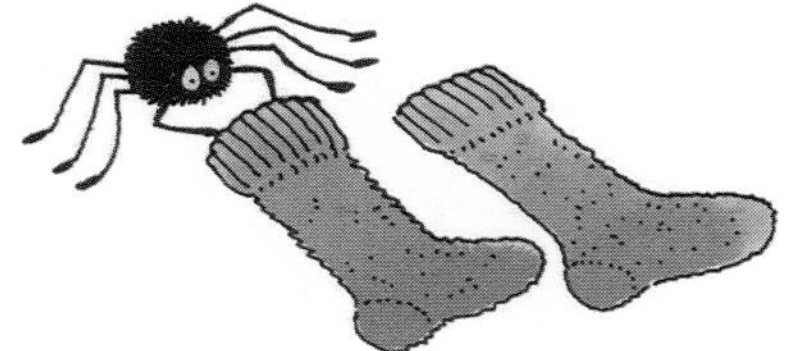

The spider has found two socks. They are a pair.

palace

The king lives in a palace.

pancake

Bill is tossing a pancake.

paper

Lily is painting on a piece of paper.

parachute

The parachute is coming down.

parents

Lily's mother and father are her parents.

park

Fifi is walking in the park.

park

Henry is parking his car.

parrot

The parrot is laughing.

party

Fifi is having a party.

pass

Henry passes Bruno. He goes past him.

passport

Ben shows his passport. He is going to another country.

path

The path goes across the field.

patient

The patient is in bed. He is in hospital.

paw

The cat is licking its paw.

pay

Fifi pays the baker for the bread. She gives him money for it.

p

pea

Lily is eating peas.

peach

Bill is eating a peach.

pear

Ben is eating a pear.

pen

Tim is writing with a pen.

pencil

Fifi is drawing with a pencil.

people

Here are five people. Who are they?

pepper

Bill puts pepper on his food.

perhaps

Perhaps it will rain. It may rain, but it's not certain to.

Perhaps he is lost. He might be lost.

Perhaps I will have an ice cream, but I am not sure.

photograph

This is a photograph of Fifi.

piano

Fritz plays the piano.

pick

The people are picking pears.

pick up

Fifi picks up a pear that she has dropped.

picnic

Bill, Ben and Fifi are having a picnic.

picture

This is a picture of the picnic.

pie

Bill is cutting the pie.

piece

Lily is eating a piece of the pie.

pig

Here is a pink pig.

pile

Henry is carrying a pile of books.

pillow

Lily has a blue pillow.

pilot

A pilot flies aeroplanes.

pin

Bill pricks Ben with a pin.

pinch

Bill pinches Ben.

pineapple

The mice are hiding behind a pineapple.

pink

The big pig is pink.

place

Ben is looking for a place to have a picnic. He is looking for somewhere to have it.

Where is my place? Where am I supposed to sit?

Here is an empty place.

plan

The builder looks at a plan of the house he is building.

plant

Henry has a big plant.

plant

He plants it in the garden.

plate

The chips are on a plate.

play

The children are playing.

pocket

There is a handkerchief in the pocket.

point

Ben is pointing at Bill.

policeman

The policeman is pointing at Bill.

polish

Fritz is polishing the table to make it shine.

polite

Bill is very polite. He is not rude.

It is polite to say "please" when you ask for something.

pond

The ducks are swimming on a pond.

pony

Henry is riding a pony. A pony is a small horse.

poor

This man is poor. He does not have much money.

pork

Fritz is eating pork. Pork is meat from a pig.

port

The ship is in the port.

postcard

Fifi is writing a postcard.

post office

Fifi is at the post office. She is buying stamps.

potato

Henry is peeling a potato.

pour

Fifi is pouring milk into Lily's bowl.

present

Henry gives Fifi a present.

pretend

Fifi is pretending to be a ghost. She acts like one.

pretty

Fifi is a pretty girl.

price

What is the price of these potatoes? How much do they cost?

prize

Henry has won a prize for coming first.

promise

Fifi promises to send Henry a postcard. She says she will definitely send him one.

Dad has promised to take us to the zoo tomorrow.

pudding

Lily likes pudding because it is sweet.

pull

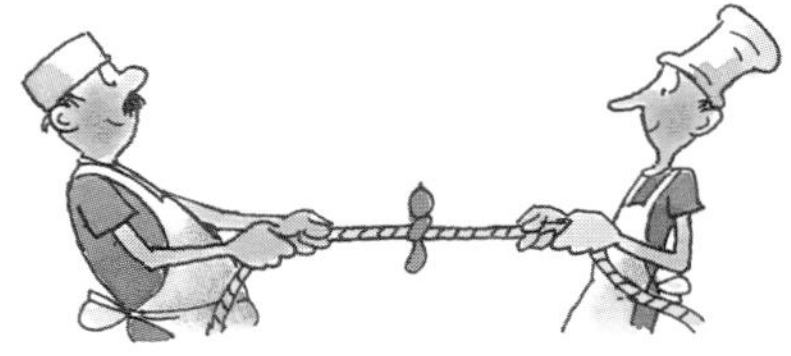

Bill and Ben are both pulling the rope.

puppet

The puppet is dancing.

puppy

A puppy is a baby dog.

purple

The king has a purple robe.

purse

Fifi puts money in her purse.

push

Bill is pushing Ben.

put

Fifi puts milk in the fridge.

puzzle

Fritz is doing a puzzle.

pyjamas

Henry is wearing pyjamas. He wears them in bed.

queen

The queen wears a crown.

question

The queen asks the king a question. She asks him something and wants him to give her an answer.

Please answer my question!

The question has no answer.

quiet

George is being very quiet. He is not making any noise.

quite

The film is quite good but the book is better.

He is quite clever. He could be more clever.

I don't quite understand what you are saying. I don't completely understand.

rabbit

The rabbit is running.

race

The rabbits are having a race. Which one will win?

radiator

The cat is sleeping by the radiator. It is warm there.

radio

Grandpa is listening to the radio.

railway line

The rabbit is sitting on the railway line.

rain

It is raining.

rainbow

There is a rainbow in the sky.

raincoat

Henry is wearing a raincoat to keep him dry.

raspberry

Here is a bowl of raspberries.

rat

The rat is chasing a rabbit.

razor

Sam shaves with a razor.

reach

Fifi cannot reach the book. It is too high.

read

Fifi is reading the book.

real

This is a real elephant. It is not a pretend one.

receive

Fifi receives a letter. The postman gives it to her.

recognize

Fritz recognizes Fifi. He knows her because he has met her before.

Do you recognize me? Can you remember who I am?

I recognize that writing. It is Fifi's writing.

record

Bill puts on a record to hear some music.

red

Fifi is painting the chair red.

refuse

The donkey refuses to move. He will not move.

remember

Fritz remembers Fifi. He has not forgotten her.

Henry cannot remember where he put his book. He has forgotten where he put it.

Can you remember your holiday last year?

rest

Henry is resting because he is tired.

ribbon

Lily is wearing a blue ribbon in her hair.

rich

This man is rich. He has a lot of money.

ride

Henry is riding a donkey.

right

Fifi raises her right hand.

ring

The lady is wearing a ring on her finger.

ring

The telephone is ringing.

river

Henry is swimming in the river.

road

There are sheep on the road.

roar

The lion is roaring. He is making a noise.

rock

Henry is sitting on a rock in the sea.

rock

George is rocking the baby.

roll

Ruff is rolling in the grass.

roof

The house has a red roof.

room

This is a room in a house.

root

The plant has long roots. They grow under the ground.

rope

Henry has climbed up a rope.

rose

Fifi is smelling a rose.

rough

The road is rough. It is not smooth.

round

The table is round. That is its shape.

row

The five pigs are standing in a row.

row

Bill is rowing a boat.

rub

The cat is rubbing its back.

run

Henry is running fast.

sack

Fred is carrying a sack.

sad

Henry is sad. He is not happy.

safe

Henry is safe. He is not in danger.

sail

Fifi is sailing a boat.

sailor

The sailor is in his boat.

salad

This is a mixed salad. It is made of raw vegetables.

salt

Bill puts salt on the salad.

same

The girls are wearing the same hat.

sand

Lily is digging in the sand.

sandal

The mouse has found a pair of sandals.

sandwich

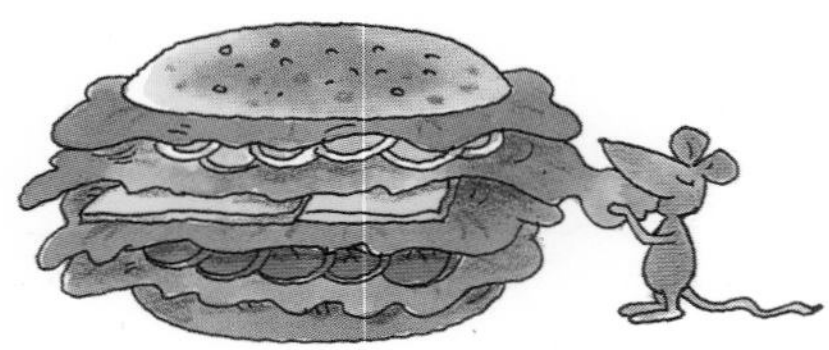

The mouse is eating a big sandwich.

sauce

Fifi is pouring sauce over the ice cream.

saucer

The cup is on a saucer.

sausage

Ben is eating sausages.

save

Fritz saved the drowning boy. He rescued him.

I would have died, but you saved my life.

Sam saved Fifi from a crocodile!

saw

Bill is sawing wood with a saw.

say

Grandpa does not say much. He does not talk much.

Bill says he is rich. He tells us he is rich.

The letter says they are well, and Fifi says they are coming next week.

scales

Fifi stands on the scales to weigh herself.

scarf

Henry has a very long scarf round his neck.

school

The children are at school.

scissors

Fifi is cutting the man's hair with a pair of scissors.

scratch

Ruff is scratching his ear.

sea

The sea is blue.

seal

The seal is swimming in the sea.

season

The four seasons of the year are spring, summer, autumn and winter.

Spring is my favourite season.

We visited Austria in the skiing season, the time of the year when you can ski.

see

Lily sees the seal. She is looking at it.

seed

Dan is sowing seeds. They will grow into plants.

seem

Dan seems to be angry. He looks as if he is angry.

sell

The baker is selling some bread to Fifi.

send

Fifi is sending a letter. She is posting it.

sentence

This is a sentence. It has four words in it.

serve

The waiter is serving Fifi. He is giving her food.

sew

Henry is sewing.

sewing machine

Sometimes he sews with a sewing machine.

shadow

Lily is looking at her shadow on the ground.

shake

Bill is shaking the tree.

shape

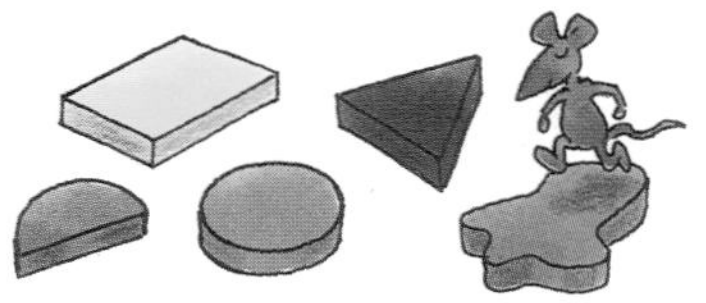

These are different shapes.

share

Bill and Ben share the cake. They each have a piece.

shark

Henry has seen the shark.

sharp

The knife is sharp. It cuts well.

sheep

The three sheep are standing in a row.

sheet

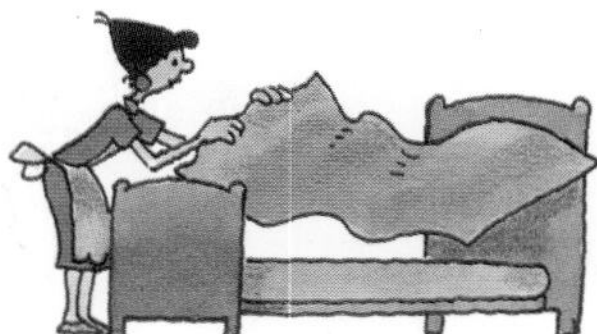

Fifi puts a sheet on the bed.

shell

Lily is holding a shell. She found it on the beach.

ship

The ship is at sea.

shirt

Fritz has a blue shirt.

shoe

The shoes are red.

short

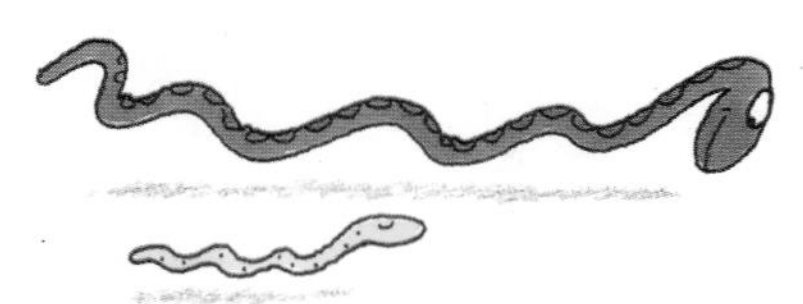

The yellow snake is short. The red snake is long.

shorts

Henry is wearing a pair of white shorts.

shoulder

The bird is sitting on the man's shoulder.

show

Fifi shows Grandpa her picture.

shower

Henry is having a shower.

shut

The gate is shut. It is not open.

side

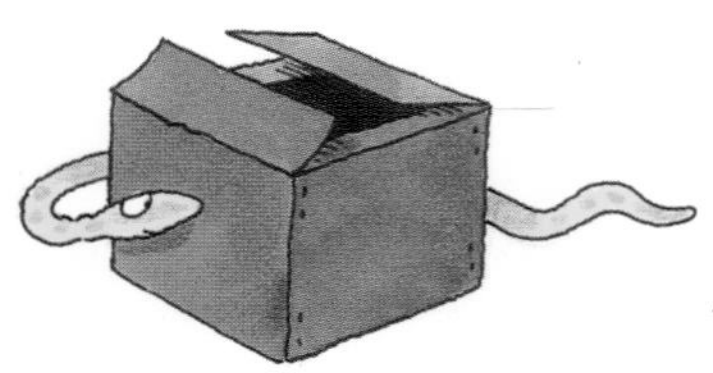

One side of the box is pink.

sign

Bill is signing a cheque. He is writing his name on it.

silver

Fifi has a silver bracelet.

since

Fifi has not seen Ben since Tuesday. Tuesday was the last time she saw him.

Since it is sunny, I will go for a walk. I will go because it is sunny.

sing

The people are singing.

sister

Lily and Daisy are sisters.

sit

Lily is sitting on a chair.

skate

Fifi and Henry are skating.

ski

Henry is putting on his skis.

ski

Henry is skiing.

skin

An elephant has grey skin.

skirt

Fifi is wearing a red skirt.

sky

The bird is in the sky. The sky is blue.

sleep

Lily is sleeping. She is not awake.

sleepy

The man is sleepy. He does not want to get up.

sleeve

The shirt only has one sleeve.

slice

Bill is cutting a slice of bread.

slide

This is a slide. It is a kind of photograph.

slide

Henry is sliding on the ice.

slipper

Lily's slippers are pink. She wears them at home.

slowly

A snail moves slowly.

small

The brown bear is small.

smell

Fifi smells the perfume. It smells nice.

smile

Fifi is smiling. She is happy.

smoke

There is smoke coming out of Henry's oven.

snail

Here is the snail again.

snake

The snake is in the grass.

snow

It is snowing. Lily is playing in the snow.

soap

Ben has soap on his face.

soccer

Sam is playing soccer. He plays with a football.

sock

Lily is wearing pink socks.

sofa

Fifi is sitting on a sofa.

soft

The cushion is soft. It is not hard.

soldier

The soldier is in the army.

some

Some of the soldiers are smiling and some are not.

someone

Someone has stolen my car.

something

There is something in my eye.

sometimes

Sometimes I am sad.

son

Henry is Grandpa's son. Grandpa is Henry's father.

song

The singer is singing a song.

soon

We will go home soon. We will go in a short time from now.

I want to go as soon as possible.

Soon we are going on holiday.

sort

Each man is wearing a different sort of hat.

soup

Henry is eating soup.

south

The bird is facing south. South is opposite north.

space

The astronaut is floating in space.

speak

Fifi is speaking to Grandpa. She is talking to him.

spell

Lily can spell her name. She knows how to write it.

spend

Ben is spending money. He is paying for things.

spider

The spider frightens Fifi.

spill

Petrol is spilling out of Henry's car.

spoon

Lily is eating with a spoon.

sport

Tennis, swimming and athletics are all sports.

People do sports to keep healthy.

Sam's favourite sport is soccer.

spot

Lily has lots of spots.

spread

Bill is spreading butter on the bread.

square

This is a square. A square is a shape.

stable

The horse lives in a stable.

stairs

Lily is going up the stairs.

stamp

There are two stamps on the envelope.

stand

Bill is standing on Ben's back.

star

The star shines in the sky at night.

start

This is the start of the race. It is about to begin.

station

The train is in the station.

statue

Henry is looking at a statue.

stay

Stay here. Do not go away.

Fifi is staying in bed. She is not getting up.

Henry is staying in Paris for a few days. He will spend a few days there.

stem

The caterpillar is on the stem of the flower.

steps

The cat is sitting on the steps.

stereo

Bill turns on the stereo.

stick

Dan is carrying sticks.

still

The cats are sitting still. They are not moving.

stir

The witch is stirring her brew.

stocking

Fifi is wearing a pair of black stockings.

stomach

Henry has a stomach ache.

stone

Lily picks up a stone on the beach.

stop

The car stops at the traffic lights.

storm

This is a storm. The weather is very bad.

story

Grandpa is reading the children an exciting story.

straight

The road is straight. It does not bend.

strawberry

Lily is eating a strawberry.

stream

Fifi is crossing a stream.

street

This is a street in a town.

string

The mouse has a piece of string.

striped

Fifi has a striped dress.

stroke

Lily is stroking Ruff.

strong

Sam is strong. He is not weak.

stupid

Henry is feeling stupid. He does not feel clever.

submarine

The submarine is underwater.

suddenly

The car stops suddenly. It stops very quickly.

sugar

Fifi is putting sugar in her tea to make it sweet.

suit

Henry is wearing a suit.

suitcase

Ben is carrying a suitcase. He is going on holiday.

sun

The sun is shining. It is a sunny day.

sunglasses

Bill is wearing a pair of sunglasses.

supermarket

Fifi is at the supermarket. She is shopping.

sure

Bill is sure he has won the game. He is certain he has won.

surprise

What a surprise for Fifi! She did not expect a party.

surround

The birds have surrounded the cat.

swallow

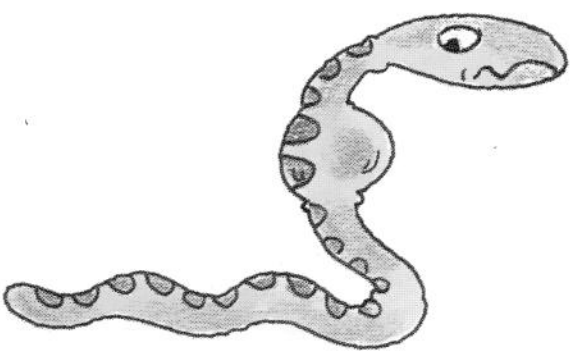

The snake has swallowed a ball. He has eaten it.

swan

The swan is swimming.

sweep

The witch is sweeping with her broom.

sweet

Lily is eating sweets.

swim

Bill and Ben are swimming.

swimming pool

The man is diving into the swimming pool.

swimsuit

Fifi has a striped swimsuit.

swing

Ben is swinging on a swing.

Tt

table

The cat is sitting on the table.

tail

One cat has a tail. The other does not.

take

Lily is taking a chocolate.

talk

The fairies are talking to each other.

t

tall

The woman is tall. The man is small.

taste

Ben is tasting the sauce to see what it is like.

taxi

Fritz hails a taxi.

tea

Fifi has a cup of tea.

teacher

The teacher is with his class. He is teaching them.

team

This is a soccer team.

teapot

Fifi is pouring the tea from the teapot.

tear

Tears run down Lily's face. She has been crying.

tear

Henry tears his trousers.

teddy bear

Lily has a teddy bear.

teeth

The rat has sharp teeth.

telephone

The telephone is ringing.

television

The children are watching television.

tell

Grandpa is telling the children an exciting story.

tennis

Bill and Ben are playing tennis.

tent

Henry is looking out of the tent.

than

Fifi is taller than her friend. He is shorter than her.

thank

Fifi thanks Ben for the present he has given her.

that

That is Henry's car, the one over there.

I would like that apple there, not this one here.

That bicycle belongs to Bill. This one is Ben's.

theatre

Fifi is at the theatre. She is watching a play.

then

He ate his dinner, then he had a piece of cake. After his dinner he had a piece of cake.

Rest first, and then go out.

We did not have a car then. We did not have one at that time.

there

The car is not there. It is not in that place.

Shall we sit here or there?

There is milk in the jug.

Is Fifi there?

thick

The slice of bread is thick. It is not thin.

thin

The man is thin. He is not fat.

thing

There are ten things on the tray. What are they?

think

Fifi is thinking about Sam.

thirsty

The man is thirsty. He wants something to drink.

this

This is my favourite painting, this one here.

This dress is pretty but that one is not.

This is an elephant and that is a camel.

thread

Fifi is sewing with cotton thread.

through

The king is coming through the door.

throw

Lily is throwing bread to the ducks.

thumb

Henry hits his thumb.

ticket

Fifi shows the conductor her ticket.

tie

Henry has a spotted tie.

tie

Bill is tying a knot in the string.

tiger

The tiger is roaring.

tights

The red tights are hanging on the line.

tired

Henry is tired. He has been running.

to

The children go to school.

Fifi is going to work.

Henry is going to the station to catch a train.

Bill gives an apple to Ben.

today

Today is Lily's birthday. It is her birthday on this day.

toe

The mouse is tickling someone's toes.

together

The cats sleep together. They sleep with each other.

tomato

Henry is slicing a tomato.

tomorrow

Tomorrow is the day after today.

Today is Monday so tomorrow will be Tuesday.

The day after tomorrow is Wednesday.

tongue

Ruff has a pink tongue.

too

The jacket is too small. It is not big enough.

tool

Here are some useful tools. They are in a tool box.

toothbrush

The mouse brings a toothbrush . . .

toothpaste

. . . and puts toothpaste on it.

top

Ben is at the top of the stepladder.

touch

Alice touches her cardigan. It feels soft.

towards

The cat is walking towards the milk.

towel

Henry is drying himself with a yellow towel.

tower

This is a famous tower. Where is it?[1]

town

This is a town. There are many houses in it.

toy

Lily is playing with a toy.

tractor

Henry is driving a tractor.

traffic lights

Henry hits the traffic lights.

train

Henry gets on a train.

tree

The tree has green leaves.

1. In Italy. It is the Leaning Tower of Pisa.

triangle

These are all triangles. A triangle is a shape.

trumpet

Ben is playing a trumpet.

try

Lily is trying to build a tower.

tulip

The tulips are in a vase.

tune

Ben is dancing to a tune on the radio.

tunnel

The train is coming out of the tunnel.

turn

The car is turning left.

twin

Bella and Betty are twins.

type

Henry is typing.

typewriter

His typewriter is very old.

ugly

The monster is ugly. He is not beautiful.

umbrella

Henry's umbrella blows away.

uncle

Tom is Lily's uncle. He is Aunt Alice's husband.

under

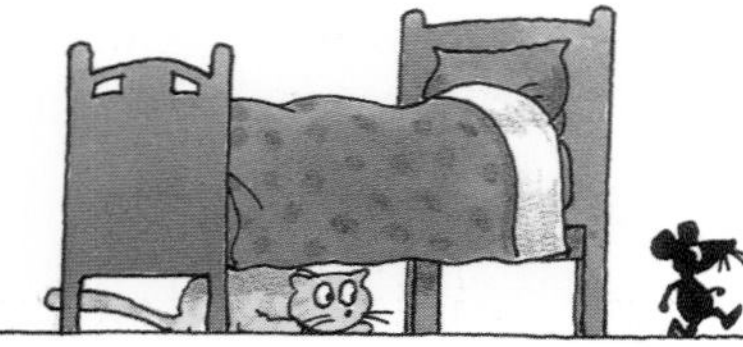

The cat is under the bed.

understand

I understand what he says. I know what he means.

I understand how this machine works. I know how it works.

I can understand French.

undress

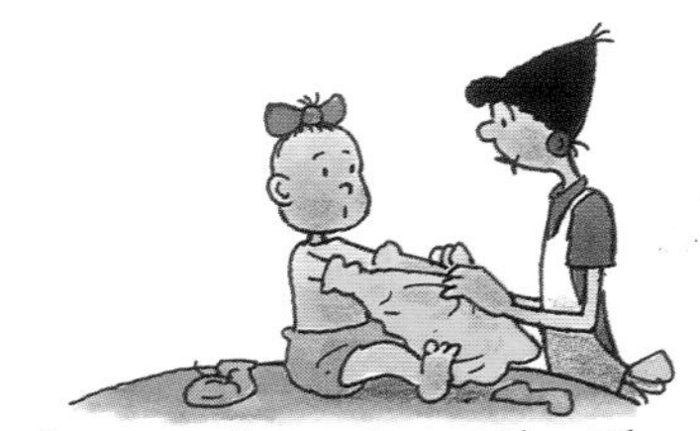

Fifi is undressing Lily. She is taking off her clothes.

unhappy

Henry is unhappy. He is not happy.

uniform

The man in the lift wears a uniform.

unless

We will swim unless it rains. Except if it rains, we will swim.

Unless I hurry I will be late.

Ben's cake will burn unless he takes it out of the oven.

until

Lily can play until six o'clock. That is the time when she must stop playing.

Wait until I come back.

Ben is not coming home until tomorrow.

up

Henry is going up a ladder. He is not going down it.

upstairs

The cat is upstairs. It is not downstairs.

use

Fifi is using a knife to cut the bread.

useful

The knife is useful. It helps Fifi cut things.

vacuum cleaner

The vacuum cleaner cleans the carpet.

valley

The river flows through the valley.

vase

The vase is full of flowers.

vegetables

These are all vegetables.

very

Ben speaks French well. Henry speaks French very well. He speaks it even better than Ben.

A mouse is small. An insect is smaller. It is very small.

village

A village is smaller than a town.

violin

Henry plays the violin.

visit

Fifi is visiting Grandpa. She has come to see him.

voice

Grandpa has a quiet voice. He speaks quietly.

Ben has a low voice and Fifi has a high voice.

When you shout, your voice gets louder.

wait

Alice is waiting for a bus.

waiter

The waiter is serving Fifi.

wake

Henry is waking up. It is morning.

walk

Fifi is going for a walk.

wall

The cats are sitting on top of the wall.

wallpaper

Bill is putting up wallpaper.

want

Lily wants a cake. She hopes she can have one.

warm

Fifi is warm. She is lying in the sun.

wash

Henry is washing his face to make it clean.

washing machine

The washing machine is on. It is washing clothes.

wasp

The wasp has stung Henry.

watch

Fifi looks at her watch to see what time it is.

watch

Fifi and Sam watch a film.

water

The water is overflowing.

waterfall

Tarzan is crossing the waterfall.

wave

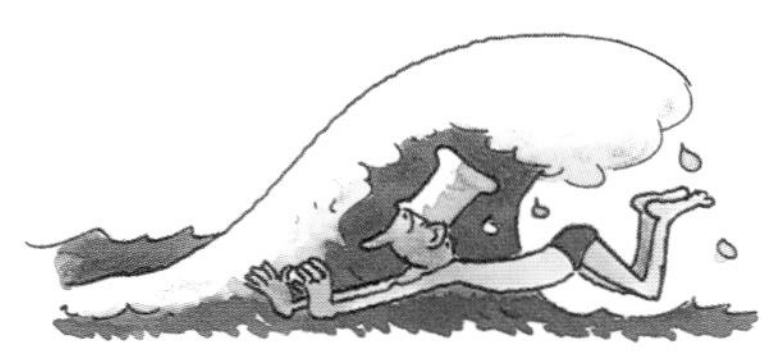

Ben dives under the wave.

way

Henry does not know which way to go.

weak

Henry is weak. He is not strong.

wear

Fifi is wearing a hat.

wedding

The bride and bridegroom are at their wedding.

weigh

Fifi is weighing the flour.

west

The bird is facing west. West is opposite east.

wet

The dog is very wet. He is not dry.

whale

The whale meets a boat.

what

What time is it?

What do you want for lunch?

Fifi does not know what Lily is doing.

wheat

Wheat is growing in the field.

wheel

The bicycle has one big wheel and one small wheel.

wheelbarrow

The wheelbarrow is full.

when

When does the train leave? At what time does it leave?

I had a car when I lived in Paris. I had a car then.

Come when you have finished. Come after you have finished.

where

Where is the cat? Can you see where it is?

which

Which cat is the biggest? Which cat is the smallest?

while

Lily dreams while she sleeps.

whisper

Fifi is whispering to Ben. She is talking quietly.

whistle

The man is blowing a whistle.

white

The fat cat is white. The thin cat is black.

who

Who is wearing a hat? Which person?

why

Why is Henry up a tree? For what reason?

wide

The river is very wide. It is not narrow.

wife

Heidi is Fritz's wife. He is her husband.

win

Sam wins the race. He finishes first.

wind

The wind is blowing.

windmill

This is a windmill.

window

Fifi leans out of the window to call Sam.

wing

The bird is flapping its wings.

wipe

Bill is wiping the table.

wire

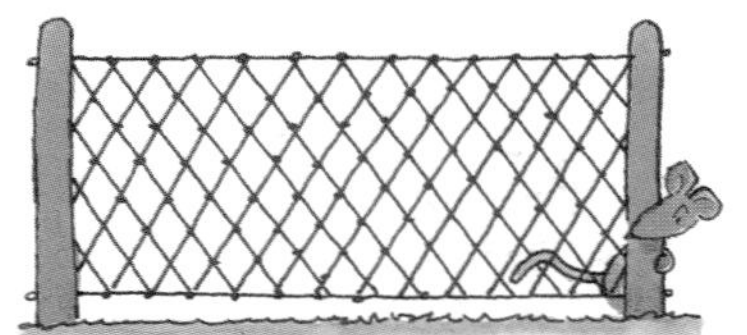

The fence is made of wire.

witch

The witch is flying.

with

She is with her cat.

without

Now she is without her cat.

woman

Fifi is a woman. Henry is a man.

wood

The table is made of wood. Wood comes from trees.

wool

Here are three balls of wool.

word

Lily is writing a word.

work

Ben is working hard.

world

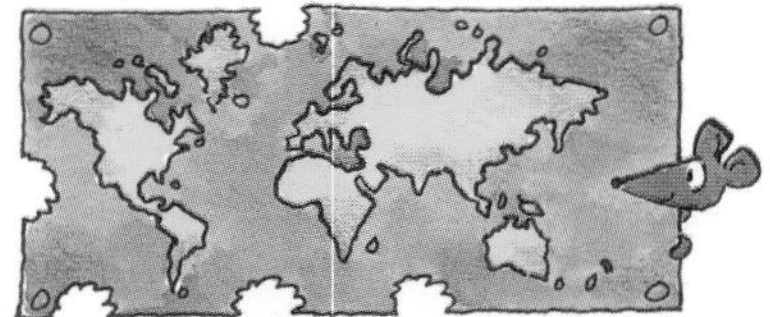

This map shows the whole world.

worm

The bird looks at the worm.

wrap

Fifi is wrapping a present.

write

Fifi is writing a letter.

wrong

The answer is wrong. It is not right.

xylophone

Fritz is playing a tune on the xylophone.

year

There are 365 days in a year.

There are 12 months or 52 weeks in a year.

There are 100 years in a century.

yellow

The chick is yellow.

yesterday

Yesterday was the day before today.

Today is Monday, yesterday was Sunday.

young

A puppy is a young dog. It is not an old dog.

zebra

A zebra has a striped coat.

zoo

Lily sees animals at the zoo. The zebra is there.

Parts of speech

In English there are several different types of word. These are usually called "parts of speech". Some of these words name things, some describe things, some are "action" words, and some join different parts of a sentence together.

It is a good idea to understand what each type of word does, because this will help you to speak and write good English. It will also help you when you learn another language. These are the eight, main types of word:

noun	A noun is a word that names a person, animal, place or thing:	**Fifi, mouse, Africa, book** **The book is on the table.**
pronoun	A pronoun is a word which takes the place of a noun. It refers to a person, animal, place or thing without giving its name:	**I, you, he, she, it, they, who, what, which** **It is on the table.**
adjective	An adjective is a word that describes a noun or pronoun:	**big, small, dangerous, new, wooden** **The book is big.**
verb	A verb is a "doing" or "action" word. It tells you what someone or something is doing:	**run, sleep, catch, eat** **Henry is running.**
adverb	An adverb is a word which describes or tells you more about a verb, an adjective or another adverb:	**quickly, soon, very, fast** **Henry is running fast.** **The man is very tall.**
preposition	A preposition tells you where people or things are in relation to each other:	**with, under, on, in** **The cat is under the table.**
conjunction	A conjunction is a link word which is used to join words or groups of words:	**and, but, when, then** **Here are Bill and Ben.** **Lily had her tea, then she went to bed.**
interjection	An interjection is an exclamation. It is usually a short word:	**Oh! Hello!** **"Oops!" said Henry.**

Useful words

Numbers

0	nought	20	twenty
1	one	21	twenty-one
2	two	22	twenty-two
3	three	23	twenty-three
4	four	24	twenty-four
5	five	25	twenty-five
6	six	26	twenty-six
7	seven	27	twenty-seven
8	eight	28	twenty-eight
9	nine	29	twenty-nine
10	ten	30	thirty
11	eleven	40	forty
12	twelve	50	fifty
13	thirteen	60	sixty
14	fourteen	70	seventy
15	fifteen	80	eighty
16	sixteen	90	ninety
17	seventeen	100	one hundred
18	eighteen	1,000	one thousand
19	nineteen	1,000,000	one million

1st	first	7th	seventh
2nd	second	8th	eighth
3rd	third	9th	ninth
4th	fourth	10th	tenth
5th	fifth	20th	twentieth
6th	sixth	50th	fiftieth

The days of the week

Monday
Tuesday
Wednesday
Thursday
Friday
Saturday
Sunday

The months of the year

January
February
March
April
May
June
July
August
September
October
November
December

The seasons

spring
summer
autumn
winter

Countries and continents

Africa
Argentina
Asia
Australia
Austria
Belgium
Brazil
Canada
China

Denmark
Egypt
England
Europe
France
Germany
Great Britain
Greece
Hungary

India
Iran
Ireland
Israel
Italy
Japan
The Netherlands
New Zealand
North America

Poland
Scotland
South America
Soviet Union
Spain
Switzerland
Turkey
United States
Wales